CAREER AS A
COURT REPORTER

TRANSCRIBE LEGAL AND BUSINESS PROCEEDINGS

CAPTION FOR TV AND THE INTERNET

ONE WAY WE LEARN IS BY THE lessons taught to us by our ancestors. The first lessons were taught by example, elders taking children out into the world and teaching by showing and doing. Later, people used verbal communication to impart lessons about how the world works and how people should behave, and pass on other stories to their young. The advancement of human learning is dependent on starting out where the last thinker left off and adding to the store of human knowledge.

This is also exactly how the legal system works. When there is a question of law, judges and attorneys look to previous legal decisions to interpret new situations. They search for and study the cases which have been decided in the past. The case law that appears in legal resource books is derived largely from the court reporter's record of the event. Court reporters create the base copy for textbooks every time they sit down at work. In the event a case is being reviewed, for example, if a person who has been convicted of a crime wants to mount an appeal of the case, the court reporter's record of the previous court proceedings is one of the first things that will be requested in researching the new case. Court reporters create and are the custodians of the living record of the law in action. They are very important to the proper functioning and integrity of the legal system.

Court reporters are also employed outside the courthouse for a variety of similar duties – it's been that way for thousands of years. An early example of someone who was in charge of keeping a running record of someone's words was a servant of the philosopher and politician Cicero. In ancient Rome, he was the most famous political thinker and orator, and when he spoke people wanted to listen. He knew this and charged his servant with taking down his words as he spoke them to be read later to people who could not witness the speech firsthand. The servant created his own notation system, the first recorded version of shorthand, and trained others to use it. It wasn't the best form of shorthand, certainly, but one of Cicero's servant's symbols – the ampersand or "and" sign which looks like & – is still in use in scores of languages around the world.

His system isn't used anymore, but the practice has gone on over the years. Starting in the 1100s, academics have created new systems of shorthand and published treatises on their use. Technology has moved the profession ahead, but the heart of the work is still centered around people writing down the spoken record for later viewing. Stenographic machines in use today, abbreviated keyboards with symbols made to be depressed simultaneously, and a process called chording, are not much removed from ones that have been used for decades. New additions have brought computerized benefits like direct to CD recording and voice-recognition software. There are new shortcuts, but nothing has replaced a court reporter at the center of the process.

All kinds of endeavors have found a meticulous record of meetings and conversations invaluable. Outside of the courtroom, legal firms hire people trained as court reporters to record depositions and statements by their clients while they research and build cases. These recordings are reliable legal records. Legal firms generate affidavits which are the basis for court actions.

Corporations and businesses use people with court reporting skills to keep records of their deliberations in meetings. Government organizations, at all levels, use court reporters to record their actions as well. On the floor of the US Senate and the US House of Representatives, there are court reporters keeping meticulous track of everything our elected officials say. The record is important. The record says what the decisions were and how the deliberative bodies came to their conclusions. Just as with their work in the courts, court reporters are an integral part of how government works.

Many court reporters work for the court system. Many more work for government agencies and large corporations. Some court reporters do not work full time for a single employer. These people who earn their living as court reporters are freelance operators who get leads from hiring agencies and go on individual assignments. Many of the organizations and governmental agencies who use court reporters don't use them every day, so they contract that work out to independent operators. These professionals are highly mobile and need to be able to navigate the different landscapes of the courtroom, the boardroom, the office and the corridors of power.

Some court reporters work in the home. Starting in Britain in the 1970s, many television broadcasts have included closed captioning for the hearing impaired. While the dialogue of a television movie or sitcom can be prepared in advance by anyone who can type, live broadcasts like the daily news and sports events require the speed and accuracy that a court reporter can provide. It's an important part of the profession, and a needed one since every television with a screen larger than 13 inches sold in the United States since 1993 has had to be able to support closed captioning viewing.

HISTORY OF THE CAREER

AS SOON AS PEOPLE WERE ABLE TO, they started recording their lives in a variety of ways. Early people passed on their experiences, their inventions and their faiths to their children, first by example and later by spoken communication. Songs, which possibly predate what we think of as speech, were created to pass on the myths, history and values of the first people. Some of those stories and themes, Sleeping Beauty, Santa Claus and even Luke Skywalker have ancient origins.

The spoken or oral tradition is unreliable, however. Anyone who has heard a rumor grow out of proportion knows that a story can be embellished even without anyone trying to change it.

Ancient people literally made their mark on the world in the early cave paintings. It was a way of imparting information that could, and has, lasted long after the creators died. Stories shift with the times and old songs take on new meanings, but the mountainside has always been the mountainside and a message left there would stand forever.

By the time the first human communities grew to the size of real cities, the importance of a written record was recognized. A hunter-gatherer society is mobile and leaves cave paintings, but they have no reason to develop a written language. The first farmers and herders didn't need to record anything. Only when humans gathered together in great numbers did writing become necessary and records vitally important.

The first written languages, hieroglyphs, were developed to manage grain stores in ancient societies. When communities grew large enough to feed themselves and store away food for the future, leaders had to come up with a way of keeping track of everything in the inventories. Leaving out the issue of trust, the amounts and locations of supplies are a life-or-death concern. A mistake or mislaying of resources can cause starvation. Keeping good records is crucial when thousands of lives are at stake. This was the birth of writing, a means to record grain stores in an accessible and understandable way.

The first instances of notes kept of conversations reaches back to the Roman era. The politician and philosopher Cicero had a servant who kept a record of the man's statements in an abbreviated fashion and used that record to carry the statements to people who could not be there at the time. The servant used a version of shorthand, one created by him, to keep a record of his master's statements – compacting words into abbreviations and relying on his understanding of context and regular uses – that allowed him to replace entire ideas with a single symbol. Cicero later came up with the practice of using three such scribes to cover a single speech and have them meet up to compare notes afterwards.

Shorthand first debuted in England in the 1100s when a monk created his own system based on lines with accent marks to denote the different letters. Passing on the knowledge, he published his system and made it available to anyone who could read. Another system was developed by an Englishman who came up with a shorthand system that did not use an alphabet. The system had 500 characters, chosen by the creator of the system, which had to be memorized. Neither of these systems is used anymore, but they are the first standardized systems of shorthand.

In the 1600s, a new system of shorthand was created, by an Englishman named Thomas Shelton, which was published for general use. After his death in 1703, the naval officer and British Member of Parliament Samuel Pepys' diary was found. Pepys' family thought the six volume collection was written in a cipher or secret code, but it was later found to be written in Shelton's shorthand as published in 1620. The diary which was not fully translated until the 1820s, stands as one of the best accounts of life in the English Restoration period.

But these instances are all in private use. The practice of making shorthand recordings as a matter of public policy came about in the late 1700s, when the government of England hired its first official shorthand writer. The man appointed used his own system and mostly employed it to keep the Houses of Parliament informed of what each other were doing. It was at this time that newspaper reporters started to use the same kinds of shorthand systems for their work. In the 1800s, new systems were developed, based on phonetics – characters and abbreviations used to stand for sounds in spoken language. The phonetic model was used almost universally for many years. The style, called Pitman after its creator Sir Isaac Pitman, is still widely used, although much changed from the original, in Great Britain and its former colonies.

In the late 1800s Robert Gregg, yet another Briton, published a book after he moved to Boston, that championed the idea of using cursive handwriting as a basis for shorthand writing – older systems used print handwriting as the form. He opened professional schools teaching his form of shorthand and the practice became so well ingrained in the business community that shorthand writing contests were held on a national level.

While any kind of organization or enterprise could benefit from shorthand, nothing warmed to it the same way the judicial system did. Courts started hiring court reporters to make real-time records of their proceedings. Court decisions can affect the lives of thousands of people. When a decision is reviewed, or studied, the court reporter's record is the primary document that is relied upon. It is essential that the document is a completely accurate account of everything that was said in the original hearing.

Shorthand using pencil and paper was soon going to go the way of the dinosaur. Even before the period of the Industrial Revolution, engineers and others at the forefront of new technology were working on the first shorthand machines. The first American patent on a shorthand machine was granted in 1879 – and it was a typewriter. The later development of the modern keyboard, the "qwerty" arrangement of a minimum of keys in a smaller space, is still in use on computer keyboards today. Interestingly, the non-alphabetical arrangement of keys was originally conceived to actually slow the typist down so that you couldn't type faster than the machine could stamp the ink ribbon.

Around the same time, the first Stenotype machines started to appear. Unlike a regular keyboard on a typewriter or computer, these machines have a much smaller number of keys made to be pressed in unison, or chording, to indicate words that come out on a rolled piece of paper like a cash register receipt. The advent of this kind of machine allowed organizations to have fast, real time and highly accurate records of conversations. Modern Stenotype machines (now computerized using stable software that stores easily and reliably and without paper) allow writers to record conversations well into the 200-words-per-minute range, faster than most people talk. The speed records on those machines are more than 370 words-per-minute.

There have been other forms of recording as well. In the 1940s, the first Stenomask devices were created out of simple materials. The modern version used today has a cone or mask with a microphone inside, which the reporter holds over his/her mouth. The reporter then "revoices" the words of the speaker being transcribed, as well as indicating any significant gestures or movements. The mask drowns out all sound other than the person talking into it, making it useful in loud places. Also, the operator cannot be heard – an ideal effect considering its use in places like courtrooms. The words of the reporter are translated by voice recognition technology and a written report is produced immediately.

Technology has progressed even beyond that level. After abortive attempts to come up with a machine that could translate foreign languages into English, early computer companies tried the less-arduous task of making a machine that could translate shorthand into Standard English. That wouldn't find a market either, but both attempts paved the way for computer aided translation.

Computer aided translation takes many different forms and comes in many different formats. Modern court reporting systems use a CAT system that includes steno machines and masks as well as computer-to-computer translation, editing by computer screen, and instantaneous printing capability.

Technology further expanded the field when closed-captioning for the hearing impaired started to appear on television broadcasts. While the stakes aren't as high when translating a sitcom for the deaf as when a recorder is transcribing a murder trial, there is still need for speed and accuracy. Court reporters are hired to provide real time closed captioning for broadcasts of all types, often working from their homes via Internet connections.

A practice that can generate national competitions can also bring into being a national organization of practitioners. Near the turn of the 20th century, the foundation of the National Shorthand Reporters Association was laid when hundreds of practitioners got together at an exposition and started talking about the need for more than just statewide organizations. Two years later, the organization was founded with 156 original members. The organization offers its members benefits, continuing education and a way to meet with others in their field. The organization changed its name late in the 20th century to the National Court Reporters Association.

WHERE YOU WILL WORK

OF THE ROUGHLY 20,000 COURT reporters working in the United States, more than half work for government at some level. The number is so high because the majority of work is for courts, legislatures and government agencies. What this means for people entering the field is that they will most likely be working in some kind of government office, either in a local unit like a city or county, or in a district court. Whether you work for a court, a city, a state or as a private contractor, court reporters are indoor employees working in an office environment.

Government offices are always highly professional environments where formal office attire is the rule. While a great majority of the working world has switched to business casual or casual Friday, government offices have resisted those changes. In a court environment, casual clothes are ruled out, usually by the judge and are not to be worn by any employees. Governmental offices are also run under different rules than regular business offices.

The regulations that govern how the government hires, disciplines and fires differ by municipality and state, and sometimes are subject to federal regulation as well.

There are, depending on the jurisdiction, possibilities for union representation and benefits. There are also pension benefits for longtime government workers. While the position of court reporter is not one traditionally affected by political patronage, other positions in government offices are, and professionals going into the field should be aware of that.

Government offices are special places that have their own rules and policies. In most cases, employees will be entrusted with pass cards or other forms of secure identification. Governmental offices are filled with important documents of all kinds, and there will likely be some kind of background check (or security clearance) for people entering the field. Almost all governmental offices are Americans with Disabilities Act compliant so they are good places of work for people with physical handicaps. They are also often secure facilities where the entrances and exits are monitored, and everyone's movements are noted. Especially in the case of a court, someone employed to do court reporting for the government is going to be working under surveillance and sometimes in the presence of armed guards.

Some reporters are hired by television stations to translate broadcasts of all kinds into closed captioning for the hearing impaired. This reporter's duty is completely out of the public's eye, and the environment is usually much more informal. These can also be union jobs, depending on the organization or corporation.

The hours are fairly standard nine-to-five. Only the busiest courts in the largest cities maintain night hours and almost none does much work on the weekends. Closed captioning work at television stations can come at any time given the event-driven nature of television news, so there is a possibility for odd-hour work there.

Legal firms keep court reporters either on staff or on retainer. Lawyers do much of their work in their offices and often need an accurate record of events. Court reporters work in legal offices taking depositions and recording other proceedings. Depositions are legal documents and the court reporter taking them down administers to the person giving testimony (the deponent) an oath as if they were in court. Legal offices come in all sizes, and the work performed there will be as diverse as the legal practices. In virtually all cases, these are professional environments so professionally appropriate attire and behavior are going to be expected.

Some court reporters are not employees. There is a market for freelance court reporters, people who will pick up piecework from referring agencies and work in a variety of venues. These reporters will have to move between courts and businesses to do their work – they'll have to be ready to work comfortably in any and all of the settings and operate just as well.

THE WORK YOU WILL DO

A COURT REPORTER MAY SPEND his/her career creating verbatim transcripts of speeches, legal proceedings, meetings, conversations and depositions for a variety of employers, both public and private. Anywhere two or more parties want a fast, accurate record of their words, a court reporter will be the standard choice for transcription of spoken communication to written words.

The most common work for court reporters is within the legal system where they are responsible for creating and maintaining an accurate legal record. The administration of the law is based on the facts, and the record of the facts (testimony, conversations between attorneys and judges, even physical movements) is vital to that process. Whenever someone speaks in court, to anyone, it is the job of the court reporter to take down every word and annotate every instruction from the judge accurately and quickly. If asked to do so by a judge, the court reporter can go back into that record during the trial to read back what was said at any particular time.

Court reporters help judges and lawyers by searching for information in the record, and they provide juries with an accurate recollection of what was said in court for their deliberations. Once a day in court is finished, it's the job of the court reporter to see to it that the record is translated from the machine shorthand or other recording devices to a written record understandable by anyone.

Court reporters are also hired or kept on retainer by courts and legal firms to take depositions from defendants, witnesses, police and other people for use in court filings. Depositions are legal documents and they are vitally important to the legal process. Court reporters are the ones who will administer an oath to the person giving testimony (tell the truth, the whole truth, etc.).

Court reporters use a variety of technologies to do their job. Stenographic transcription employs a stenotype machine to document all proceedings. The machine allows the reporter to push multiple keys at once, each combination representing different sounds or words. The symbols are later translated into text by a process called computer aided transcription, or CAT. Real time court reporters can use the stenotype and link it to a computer for real time translation and captioning.

There is also electronic reporting – using audio equipment to record court proceedings. The reporter takes notes to keep track of speakers and other events in the courtrooms, to match them up with the recorded words. The reporter also takes notes on anything that may not have been clearly recorded by the equipment (if a witness answers too quietly or mumbles, for example). The recordings are later transcribed to text.

Voice writing is done when the voice reporter repeats all

testimony into a voice silencer, which looks like a hand held mask, using a microphone inside. The mask keeps the reporter's voice from being heard in court and prevents ambient sounds from contaminating the recording being made. After court, the court reporter goes back over the recording to make the final text record of the meeting or proceeding.

After reporting in court, in government offices or in legal firms, the court reporter's job is to make a readable transcript of the day's proceedings. What comes out of a stenography machine is in a kind of code, a paper strip with a series of arcane symbols, prefixes and suffixes that only someone trained in their use can read. This is not the official record. The court reporter takes that cipher and translates it back into regular language and that becomes the record. While they are translating their notes, it's up to them to make sure the result is readable and accurate.

Court reporters also develop storage and filing systems for easy retrieval of records and original voice recordings or stenographic notes. Just as they provide the official record of proceedings in courts, offices and government bodies, they manage those recordings for future reference. In this way the court reporter is also like a librarian. After a trial, perhaps years afterward, those records can be vital to court proceedings such as an appeal or a review. Court reporters have to be able to manage recordings, voice and printed data, so they are available to those people whose work depends on them.

Outside of a court setting, there are many organizations and entities that benefit from real-time accurate transcriptions. Webcasters record press conferences for reporting on websites and blogs. Corporations and other large businesses have a need to record meetings with their staffs, and shareholder meetings for public companies that are traded on the stock market. The companies that hold technical seminars – either at trade shows or professional organization conventions – will make transcripts of their events for future use, to provide them to their attendees as a courtesy, or send them to people who could not attend in person. Businesses and schools who utilize the Internet for distance learning use court reporters to create transcripts for their students and translate spoken information to text for those students who are hearing impaired. The advent of the Internet has allowed organizations to transmit their meetings instantly to interested parties who log in to participate or read the information.

Governmental organizations at all levels utilize court reporters to record meetings. Governments keep records of everything they do, every decision they make, who argued the points and where all the money is being spent. While the numbers are found in a budget, there are also records of the deliberations and actions that led up to decisions on policies. Governmental bodies also hold hearings, the same as courts do, and they use court reporters to achieve the same level of accuracy and speed in their verbatim recordings. As with their legal duties, court reporters working for state and federal agencies are responsible for translation of those conversations, their safe and orderly keeping, and providing copies for whoever asks for them.

Television broadcasters and, increasingly, web-based broadcasters use court reporters to provide closed-captioning for the hearing impaired, the black-bordered text that appears across the bottom of a television broadcast. Those reporters use a variety of technologies to bring fast and accurate transcription of local and national news broadcasts to viewers who cannot hear the audio portion of the broadcast. Increasingly, television stations are looking for professionals who can work in Spanish, the fastest-growing language in the country.

COURT REPORTERS TALK ABOUT THEIR WORK

I Am a Court Reporter Working for a Firm That Contracts My Work to Courts and Governmental Agencies

"My firm sends me and other court reporters to work in courtrooms in five area counties where it has contracts. I very much like this aspect of the firm. It means that I don't have to report to the same office and see the exact same people day after day. Sometimes it means I have to drive further to get to the job – and you can't be late to any courtroom – but I consider that to be a bonus from time to time.

I'll work through the morning on the court's business that day which includes mostly procedural stuff, even before an actual case starts. I'll listen to and record the case and take my notes home at the end of the day. Usually, I'll do a couple of hours of work every night to get myself up to speed.

You have to be dedicated to doing a good job. Your mind can't wander for a second when there's business before the court. If you're not paying attention for even a short period of time you can lose the thread of the conversation and have to interrupt the court to catch up. That's not good. I like to spend a few minutes before going into court to get my mind on the right track, to get my head in the right place for doing the recording. It's the ability to focus and keep focused that is the difference between doing well on the job and really struggling.

I use a computerized recording device that puts everything onto a CD that we key in after the day's proceedings are over. We used to use an old fashioned reel-to-reel recorder but that had its own problems. Every now and again you would have to change the tape. Even when they came out with reliable cassette tapes there would come a time when you had to switch out the old tape and put in a new one. With those formats, it was always a good idea to take shorthand notes while the tape was running. I still do.

The devices we use now are better because we can isolate single voices to play back, or instantly go back through the records for months or even years if we have to. The technology makes things easier, but there still needs to be a person there. The machines can only take you so far, the rest of the process requires a trained operator.

When I need to transcribe a court session into text I end up listening to the whole trial again. The way things work in the firm that employs me is there is a proofreader who goes over everything I've keyed into text to check for misspellings and other problems. If there's an appeal of a trial, we have just 60 days to get the whole trial on paper, and that's only if the decision to appeal is made immediately. Each hour of testimony in court turns out to be about 50 pages of typed text."

I Am a Freelance Court Reporter

"I get most of my jobs through the state, so I spend the majority of my time in the capitol building making records of hearings by a number of different government agencies and boards. That keeps this job very interesting for me because I'm always in a different room hearing about different things. I consider that to be one of the great bonuses of my job. I'm always learning about new things from people who are the experts in their fields. I'm very up on current events in the state as a result.

I sit there at a special desk in the front of the room (by myself) where I can easily hear whoever is talking, be they on my right from a state agency or on my left where members of the public stand at a podium to give their viewpoints and add testimony to the record. It's my job to make sure that every single word spoken by every single person in the room is quickly and accurately taken down. I get to stop the proceedings if there's something I didn't quite hear correctly or didn't understand.

I use a machine that has an abbreviated keyboard marked in symbols that stand for sounds common in the language that I turn into real text later on. There are a whole host of different keystrokes that can be used to designate common phrases or often-used terms. Things like 'chairman,' phrases like 'through the chair and to you,' or an individual person's name will come up very often so they get
abbreviated. Specialized ones are used when a particular phrase becomes common enough within the courtroom. This is the same process as it is in news reporting, "weapons of mass destruction" quickly became "wmds" after they were mentioned enough times. What comes out of the machine isn't readable to anyone who doesn't know how to read it, so someone who is trained in its use is necessary to translate it into readable English.

After all the proceedings are completed, I take my

transcripts and turn them into readable copy. I check my work for errors in spelling or grammar. That's not always so important – what's most important is that all the words that were said are in the completed text. After I'm done I send the transcript to the agency for a final proofread by someone else. It's a good thing to have someone else look over the record before it's filed away or given out to someone on request. You can't always see errors in your own work; a second set of eyes on the product is a good thing and makes a better record."

I Am a Court Reporter Working for a District Court

"I have been working here for 15 years and have worked mainly with the same two judges in that time. There are judges that come in from other courts from time to time, filling in for one another, but there have only been two on the bench here full time. Attorneys don't like to run against sitting judges, so generally you don't see a new judge until someone is ready to retire.

Even then, judges do come and go, but there are always going to be court reporters working in the court system. There have been many labor saving devices introduced over the years and they're always getting better, but nothing is going to replace a person taking down the day's proceedings at the side of the judge. That's not going to change.

They used to think that a tape recorder was going to replace us in the room, but that didn't work. A tape recorder can't stop the court to clarify what someone said, and it can't always recognized the difference between two speakers with similar voices. It's the same thing with the new CAT technology. It's nice to have all of your work going onto a CD and through a computer that picks up your words, but that is no substitute for a live person running the machine. The best voice recognition software is usually accurate but it has its limitations. Even the best software is for a single user. The program takes a while to 'get used' to a person's speech patterns. That makes it good for a court reporter or someone who is trying to write something without the use of their hands – but again only that person. The software is useless when it has to handle a roomful of people talking, which is the environment you get in court.

So you have people working with Stenomasks connected to computers running those programs, but they're still court reporters. As the courtroom proceedings go on, they're speaking into the mask, repeating every word that's said, and the program is turning that voice into text on a screen. You still need a trained person to be able to run the machine, someone able to spot when the machine is failing to get the words accurately, and someone who can repeat that testimony back when the judge wants it. I think people prefer a live reporter to a machine, whether they notice it or not."

PERSONAL QUALIFICATIONS

COURT REPORTERS HAVE TO BE hard working, attentive people. A court reporter has to have excellent hearing and a good facility for keeping track of several lines of conversation at once. In a court setting, court reporters have to be listening to the judge, the lawyers, the witnesses and the court officers, and be accurately reporting everything they say and do all at the same time.

Court reporters also need to have writing skills. They are not called on to describe the situations going on in the court – only the conversations, but they have to be able to turn their notes into understandable language. A court reporter has to have sufficient writing ability to transform the conversations and deliberations of the courtroom into written text. The spelling, grammar and usage the reporter uses must be spot-on perfect. Of course, whoever reads a court transcript will have to understand the law and legal terminology to fully interpret the transcript, but no one should have to struggle with unclear copy or vague wordings.

Court reporters also have to understand how to operate their machines – the steno machine, computerized transcription platforms, digital tape – perfectly and without hitches. People working in the field need to be able to identify possible problems with their technology and be able to repair or recommend replacing the needed pieces immediately. They also have to know the software used for each computerized program they utilize.

Professional work environment skills are important too. Court reporters work in highly specialized environments, working on very important issues with very important people. Courts are where the law of the land is administered and there is no room for someone who is not serious about the process. Judges are typically highly educated and highly dedicated people doing very serious jobs. Attorneys are also highly educated people who expect a level of professionalism from the people they work with, and they will not long tolerate shoddy work or lax attitudes. This is also true of government work. Elected officials are doing the public's work every day and they will require the people recording their deliberations to be professional and dedicated.

Court reporters also have to be mindful of egos and personalities in their workplace. Judges, attorneys and elected officials generally expect a certain deference from those people they employ. People who record the proceedings they put on have to be aware that their employers may have inflated self images. Many of them will be elected officials and they may believe they have mandates to act as they choose. At the same time, court reporters have to be able to tell these people to stop what they're doing and clarify what they've said if there is a question in transcription.

ATTRACTIVE FEATURES

THERE ARE NUMEROUS BENEFITS TO working in this field. Court reporters are, in many cases, government employees and can benefit from the same kinds of incentive packages offered to other government workers. Generally, government workers get many paid holidays. Whenever city hall or the Post Office is closed, court reporters working for governments are going to have the day off as well.

This also means that court reporters working in the public sector can have access to union benefits. Sometimes they'll be grouped with office and clerical workers, other times they'll be in the same pool of workers that includes the police, fire fighters and sanitation workers. With union membership – depending on the state and the municipality – comes health benefits, wage guarantees, retirement savings plans and grievance resolution mechanisms.

Another positive about court reporting, and most government work, is that it is very stable. Court reporters working in the public sector can expect to work the same number of hours, week in and week out, and also can expect to have solid employment. They will work in a professional, secure environment. The circles court reporters move in are courts, government offices and legal offices – professional environments where behavior is tightly regulated. Those who are concerned about safety in the workplace should appreciate that court reporters often work in environments that have multiple safeguards on entrances and, at times, armed guards in full view. It also should be mentioned that court reporters working in the legal field and government offices will have chances to get to know very influential people with access to the levers of power. It's not exaggerating to say that making connections on that level can have its own benefits.

Court reporting skills are also very portable. Someone who works in a courtroom in California can get the same job doing the same thing in Rhode Island – the job does not differ from place to place. The skills that work in the courtroom will work just as well in government offices and corporate boardrooms – even the technology used is the same in most cases. There are of course some differences, jargon and terminology differ among highly specialized professions, but the act of taking down conversations is very much the same from one place to another.

Freelance court reporters can enjoy greater flexibility than their full-time counterparts and can to a great degree manage how their days will flow. This is a good work environment for people who are positive self starters, or for those who are managing other concerns like families. Freelance court reporters also get to work in a variety of venues. Sometimes they'll work in a courtroom, other times they'll be working in the well of a legislative body or in a corporate boardroom. They'll be able to finish their work from the comfort of their home offices. For those people who like a bit more variety in their working environment, freelance court reporting for a referring firm is a good choice.

NEGATIVE FACTORS

THE WORK OF COURT REPORTERS must be meticulously accurate. Because court proceedings are so important – they often decide whether or not a defendant will be confined in prison or fined thousands of dollars – the work there can be stressful. A mistake in recording proceedings of the judges, attorneys or witnesses could cost a plaintiff or defendant dearly. People who are not ready or are incapable of handling that kind of responsibility will not do well in this career.

Court reporters will need to study the disciplines they are called upon to record. Reporters don't have to be lawyers, of course, but it would certainly help them to know the kinds of legal jargon they are called upon to transcribe. Much of what helps a court reporter to do the job well is an ability to recognize quickly repeated, common phrases and find a way to abbreviate them for use in notes. Similarly, those people working as stenographers in the medical field will have to deal with some highly complex and highly specialized terminology, and will have to dedicate time to learning the correct spelling and meaning of these nonstandard words.

The job is also subject to deadline pressure. After a trial is adjourned, the court reporter has to turn notes of that day into readable text in a limited amount of time. If that deadline isn't met, for whatever reason, the court reporter is the one held responsible. Similarly, you are responsible for the management of court records, even those that were generated long before you were working there. If something is required and cannot be located, it's your responsibility.

Court reporters are not mere microphones; they are doing more than just transcribing conversations. While testimony is going on in a courtroom, it is the court reporter's job to get that testimony recorded correctly while it is happening. If there is a question about precisely what was said or who said it, the court reporter has to speak up, stop the proceedings and get the record straight. To do this job, you can't have a problem with interrupting powerful people in authority.

Court reporters deal on a daily basis with some fairly high powered personalities. Judges, who are either elected or appointed, demand a level of deference and respect that most employees don't have to give the boss. Politicians and government officials can have an inflated view of themselves and can be difficult personalities to manage. People who are not able to deal effectively with these kinds of personalities and egos might want to reconsider this job path.

When doing actual work, court reporters are sitting still at a desk, either speaking into a voice recorder or operating a steno machine. In the case of a reporter recording proceedings in a court of law or in the well of a legislative body, he/she may be required to sit still for a very long time. Court reporters are susceptible to contracting workplace related injuries like carpal tunnel disorder or repetitive stress disorder. At the least, you may become stiff and sore from so many hours in one stationary position.

EDUCATION

HOW MUCH EDUCATION AN aspiring court reporter needs to get depends on what kind of reporting you want to start doing. A year's training can prepare someone to be a novice voice writer, a job you can hold on an intern basis while getting further training and on-the-job experience. It takes twice as long to become fully conversant with real time voice writing. A professional real time stenographer will have been working on the machine for almost three years.

Courses in these skills are available in community colleges and, in some communities, post-secondary adult learning annexes and job retraining programs. The basic courses are offered as part of general business education courses and are available almost everywhere in the country. Typing classes are given at the high school level, and you should definitely become an expert typist. Also, court reporters have to be able to spell, and have a strong vocabulary, strong grammar, and accurate punctuation.

A note about vocabulary: Court reporters will need a good

understanding of legal terms and jargon. For those who intend to work in a court of law, this is a must. The same goes for people doing transcriptions for the medical field. If anything, the vocabulary requirements in the medical field are more difficult, since many of the words used are not in common usage.

The National Court Reporters Association has a list of programs around the country that offer the specific training a professional, accredited court reporter will need to be in line with their standards. People looking to get into these programs will have to be able to record at a specified minimum number of words per minute, so prior training is necessary. You can find the school list organized according to state at:

http://www.ncra.org/Education/content.cfm?ItemNumber=8511 &navItemNumber=11551

Licensing

For some jobs and in some states, candidates will have to pursue a license. The National Verbatim Reporters Association has three different license categories: the Certified Verbatim Reporter, the Certificate of Merit, and the Real Time Verbatim Reporter certification. The first license calls for a written test with punctuation and spelling elements. There is also a typing test that gauges speed and accuracy. The Certificate of Merit also checks for speed and accuracy, but at a higher level of difficulty. The Real Time Verbatim Reporter license calls for a test of real-time transcription and reporting. It also tests captioning, court work and web work. These licenses are generally accepted as state licensing in those states that have a requirement.

The National Court Reporters Association also offers professional licensing. Basic level members can get the Registered Professional Reporter classification by taking a test and committing to continuing education. The further certifications, including Registered Merit Reporter and Registered Diplomatic Reporter, designate higher levels of ability. The organization also offers certifications for work in broadcasting (Certified Broadcast Captioner) and online (Certified CART Provider).

EARNINGS

COURT REPORTERS CAN EXPECT TO make about $45,000 per year (about $22 per hour) based on the national average. Most earn between $30,000 and $60,000 a year. The lowest paid are around $25,000, while the highest earnings can reach $80,000 per year.

Those court reporters working in the judicial system and for governments make on average about $45,000 a year, and those working for business concerns make on average about $40,000 per year. Freelance court reporters are paid by the page recorded and also another per page fee for records they transcribe.

Those are some wide-ranging salaries, but it's important to know that earnings differ from person to person as much as they do from employer to employer. The biggest factor in determining how much a person can expect to make is based on ability. Those professionals who are doing the best work, the fastest transcription with the fewest number of mistakes per page, are going to make the best money. The record for court reporting transcription is 245 words per minute with better than 90 percent accuracy. For those keeping track, 245 words per minute is faster than an auctioneer can bark out bids at a state fair.

The amount of money one can expect to make is also affected by one's level of certification or license from any of the court reporters' national associations. The National Court Reporters Association, the American Association of Electronic Reporters and Transcribers, the United States Court Reporters Association and the National Verbatim Court Reporters association all offer various levels of certification for their members. Indeed, membership in any of these organizations requires that members keep up on new technologies and practices. The level of certification in those organizations is factored in when employers calculate earnings for a new employee.

Other compensation in the form of fringe benefits can vary widely depending on the employer. In many cases, for court and government employees, court reporters are included in the benefits packages afforded other clerical workers in the system. In other situations, court reporters can become part of existing municipal labor unions and get their benefits based on length of time working, level of expertise, and other factors. Union representation also gives the benefit of a grievance process for workplace issues and negotiation practices for situations ranging from flextime usage to collective bargaining.

Court reporters working for legal firms or corporations will also likely fit into existing health, retirement and pay packages, and those will vary from company to company.

Freelance court reporters will have to come up with health plans and retirement packages to fill their own needs, while court reporters working for municipalities, courts and state and federal governmental units will most often find their benefits packages already set when they start work.

OPPORTUNITIES

THERE ARE ABOUT 20,000 COURT reporters working in some capacity in the United States today, with just more than half of them working in either the judicial system or in government (state legislatures, etc.) exclusively.

The future for court reporters is fairly bright with the number of new positions in the field likely to rise through the coming decade. The growth for positions in the field will go on in all sectors. Government, which has always used court reporters to record their actions, will likely need more people to transcribe their proceedings as the new media, especially the Internet, continue to grow. As more and more websites proliferate that are watchdogs of government, there will be a greater need for professionals to transcribe and manage the copious logs of governmental proceedings.

The operation of courts and police departments is not normally affected by recessions and economic downturns. When the economy is going well, courts have a need to report what they do for a permanent record, and jobs there will be secure. When the economy turns sour, police say that crime goes up and therefore there will be an increasing need for court services of all kinds moving ahead.

In television, the need for real-time transcription for closed captioning is going to rise. The number of American households served by cable or other pay television services (satellite or telephone based service) is already over 50 percent. As more of these television services become available in rural areas, the need for closed-captioning services is going to go up for everything from local news broadcasts to cable-access programming. Along the same lines, local governmental agencies (townships, small cities) more and more have their own cable channels dedicated exclusively to local programming. They will need real time transcription for their municipal meetings and whatever other local programming they create on their own.

There is also a growing market for Spanish language transcription.

There will be an increasing need for people with real-time transcription skills working to put copy onto the Internet. Like the work of court reporters in the television industry, the Internet is creating a new wealth of jobs putting new content out onto the web. Many of these jobs will be in small operations with fewer than 10 employees, but that will change as Internet usage rises in coming years. As time goes on, more and more people with court reporter's skills can expect to find freelance and full-time work in companies that serve the World Wide Web.

GETTING STARTED

STARTING A CAREER AS A COURT reporter can be done anywhere, as the basic training begins in high school with writing, grammar and composition classes.

Classes in operation of a steno machine and the taking of shorthand can be picked up at community colleges and also at adult extension or learning annex courses anywhere in the country. For official court reporter training, there are post-secondary vocational and technical schools offering courses in the field.

People going into court reporting should remember that the job is learned primarily by doing. There are many opportunities to learn about how to use the various machines, but nothing will take the place of real experience in recording and transcribing conversations in real time. If someone is working for a private company, you'll also likely learn on the job under the supervision of a more senior employee at the company. The standard for ability is to be able to capture 225 words per minute – this is also a benchmark used by the federal government for employment as a court reporter.

People taking accredited classes can expect to spend at least two years becoming a real-time voice writer and another approximately 33 months to become a proficient real-time steno typist. The National Court Reporters Association NCRA has certified 70 programs in those disciplines and calls for successful completion of a four part examination. Getting that certification is conditional on further study, as members of the organization must participate in continuing education classes to show they are not only keeping up their skills but are also aware of and up to date on the newest advances in techniques and technology.

The continuing education element of the NCRA is a good thing, as some states require voice writers to be licensed in order to get work, but they are by no means the only organization serving the needs of court reporters. Some states require every court reporter to also get certification as a Notary Public. Most of the states that require certification look on the NCRA and other court reporter organizations' certification as good enough for their purposes, although other testing may be required. For many jobs in state and federal government, the civil service exam is required before placement at any level.

The National Verbatim Reporters Association offers three national certifications to voice writers: Certified Verbatim Reporter (CVR), Certificate of Merit (CM), and Real-Time Verbatim Reporter (RVR). For the CVR you must pass a written test, which includes spelling, punctuation, vocabulary and legal and medical terminology. The tests include three five-minute dictation exams that not only gauge a person's speed with the technology but also accuracy.

The CM certification requires the court reporter to have additional levels of speed and accuracy beyond the other tests. RVR measures skill in real time transcription, judicial reporting, CART provision and closed captioning for broadcast television. The test has moved with the times to include transcriptions for use on the Internet as part of the webcast of special events.

The United States Court Reporters Association offers voluntary certification as Federal Certified Realtime Reporter (FCRR), for court reporters working in federal courts. The exam tests basic skills of real-time reporting.

The American Association of Electronic Reporters and Transcribers (AAERT) certifies electronic and court reporters and the exam has both written and practical portions. That test is different from the others in that candidates may take the exam after two years of court reporting or transcription work.

ASSOCIATIONS

- **National Association of Court Reporters**

  http://www.ncraonline.org/

- **United States Court Reporters Association (there are also several state-based court reporters associations)**

  http://www.uscra.org/

- **American Association of Electronic Court Reporters and Transcriber**

  http://www.aaert.org/

- **National Verbatim Reporters Association**

  http://www.nvra.org/

www.ingramcontent.com/pod-product-compliance
Lightning Source LLC
Chambersburg PA
CBHW070755180526
45168CB00004B/1624